KNIGHTS AND CASTLES

Jackie Gaff

p

CONTENTS

This is a Parragon Publishing Book
First published in 2002

Parragon Publishing
Queen Street House
4 Queen Street
Bath BA1 1HE, UK

Produced by

David West ☆ Children's Books
7 Princeton Court
55 Felsham Road
Putney
London SW15 1AZ, UK

British Library Cataloguing-in-Publication Data

A catalogue record for this book is available from
the British Library.

ISBN 0-75257-828-6

Printed in Dubai

Designers
Julie Joubinaux, Rob Shone

Illustrator
James Field (SGA)

Cartoonist
Peter Wilks (SGA)

Editor
James Pickering

THE FIRST CASTLES

WHEN THE FIRST CASTLES were built in Europe about 1,000 years ago, they were nothing more than wooden buildings surrounded by tall fences. They were called motte-and-bailey castles.

The motte was a large mound of earth, and the bailey was the yard below. The fence around the castle was called a palisade. Outside the palisade there was often a water-filled ditch called a moat.

Safe as houses
There was often a main building called the hall inside the bailey, as well as stables, storehouses and a well for water. If enemies attacked, the safest place was the tower on top of the motte.

YOU MUST BE JOKING!
A castle is a fortified building – one that's been strengthened to protect it from attack. Castles were not the first fortified structures, though. Since prehistoric times, people had been building sturdy fences or walls to protect their villages.

THE NORMAN CONQUEST

In 1066, the English were conquered at the Battle of Hastings by the Normans, who invaded from Normandy, in France. The Normans were great castle builders and, to back up their conquest, they built motte-and-bailey castles throughout England.

CAN YOU BELIEVE IT?
Motte-and-bailey castles could be built within weeks.

YES. They were much quicker and cheaper to build than a stone castle.

FOR SALE

THE **GREAT AGE** of castle building lasted for about 500 years. For much of this time Europe was divided into many kingdoms, with the kings fighting one another to win more land and power.

Kings on top
The king was the most powerful person in a kingdom. Below him came his lords and powerful churchmen (bishops and abbots). Below the lords came their knights. The system of giving land in return for loyalty is called feudalism.

YOU MUST BE JOKING!
Land was power in castle times, and a castle was a stronghold from which land could be controlled and defended. It was also a home for the lord and his family, knights, soldiers and servants.

Each king needed his lords' support to help him fight, and he allowed lords to hold land in return for backing him. In his turn, each lord was supported by his own knights and soldiers. Knights were warriors who fought on horseback, and some were rewarded with areas of their lord's land.

CAN YOU BELIEVE IT?
Kings didn't own castles.

NO. Some kings had lots. By 1214, for example, King John of England had more than 100 castles.

BOTTOM OF THE HEAP
The lowest of the low in castle times were the peasants who worked the land. Some peasants were freemen and women, but others were slaves called villeins. In times of war, freemen and villeins had to fight in their lord's army.

STONE BUILDINGS are stronger than wooden ones, and harder for enemies to burn down. So motte-and-bailey castles were gradually replaced by stone ones.

By the middle of the 12th century, the fashion was to build a tall square or rectangular stone tower called a keep. Sometimes, the keep was surrounded by a sturdy stone wall and a moat.

Keeping safe
In a large keep, storerooms and dungeons were often in the basement. The kitchen and soldiers' barracks were on the ground floor. Next came the main living area, the great hall, and above it the lord's apartments.

Kitchens

Storeroom

CAN YOU BELIEVE IT?
Castle walls were dozens of feet thick.

NO. They were usually 6 to 16 feet thick.

WALLS OF STRENGTH

By the 13th century, castle builders were concentrating on walls. Living and working quarters were in the buildings that lined the walls, and the towers set into them. A gatehouse guarded the main entrance. Concentric castles were protected by two rings of walls.

Living and working area

Keep

Gatehouse

Outer wall

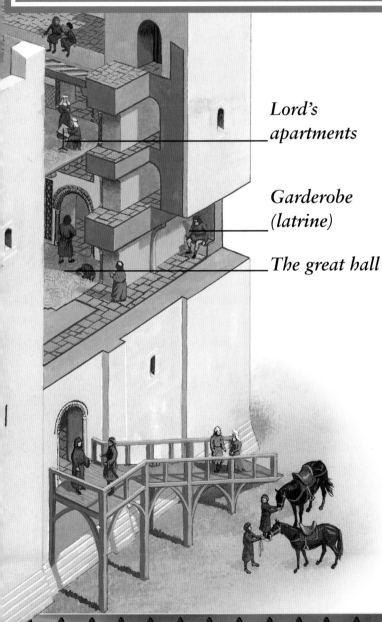

Lord's apartments

Garderobe (latrine)

The great hall

YOU MUST BE JOKING!

Castle stairs were built to wind up to the right. This meant that the sword arm of a righthanded defender coming down the stairs was free – unlike that of an attacker coming up the stairs.

SIEGE WARFARE

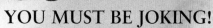

ONCE YOU'D LAID SIEGE to a castle – surrounding it with your army and trapping everyone inside – there were two main ways to capture it. One was to wait until the people inside ran out of food and water, and were forced to surrender.

YOU MUST BE JOKING! Cannon were first used in European siege warfare during the 14th century. The biggest cannon were called bombards, and they could hurl a 770-lb stone ball – as heavy as four men.

The other was to try to force your way over or through the walls!

CAN YOU BELIEVE IT? *Siege catapults were only used to hurl rocks.*

NO. Beehives and rotting animal carcasses were also shot toward the enemy.

Siege engines
Attackers used ladders and tall siege towers to try to scale the walls. Giant catapults called trebuchets and mangonels were used to hurl rocks. A springald was a huge crossbow.

UNDERMINING THE WALLS

Attackers would also try to tunnel under the castle walls. Tunnelers used wooden props to hold up the tunnel roof. When they were under the main wall, they set the props on fire – hoping that when the props burnt away, the tunnel and the wall above would collapse.

Castle wall _____

Tunnel

DEFENSE TACTICS

THE FIRST THING YOU DID when you spotted an enemy heading toward your castle was to pull up the drawbridge to close off the main entrance. Then you'd set your carpenters to work, building wooden structures called hoardings around the top of the castle towers and walls. The hoardings jutted out, so missiles could be dropped through on to enemies trying to scale the walls.

GUARDING THE GATEHOUSE

Behind the gatehouse's raised drawbridge, there were often several sets of doors, including a grill called a portcullis. In the ceiling above the main passage there were openings called murder holes, for dropping missiles on to attackers.

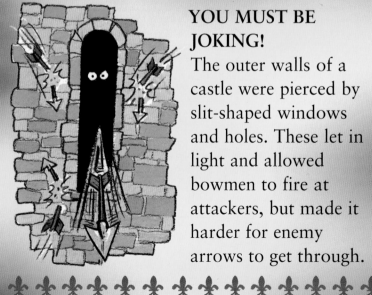

YOU MUST BE JOKING!

The outer walls of a castle were pierced by slit-shaped windows and holes. These let in light and allowed bowmen to fire at attackers, but made it harder for enemy arrows to get through.

CAN YOU BELIEVE IT?
Portcullises were made of solid iron.

NO. They were made of wood which was covered in iron sheeting.

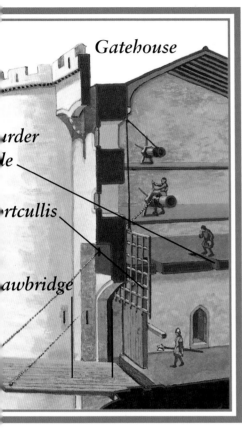

Gatehouse

urder
le

rtcullis

awbridge

Hoarding up trouble

Castle defenders dropped
rocks and boiling oil through
holes in the bottom of the
hoardings. Roofs, hoardings
and other wooden structures
were covered in water-
soaked animal hides to
protect them from fire.

13

KNIGHTS IN ARMOR

NOT ALL BATTLES were sieges, and many were fought out in open country by two opposing armies. Knights charged into battle on horseback, pointing a long spear called a lance at their enemy.

Then they switched to another weapon. This might be an ax, a dagger or a mace – a club tipped by a heavy metal ball which was often spiked. A knight's favorite weapon, however, was his sword.

Protective cover
Armor helped to protect a knight and his horse from the enemy's weapons. The knight's warhorse was about the same size as a modernday showjumper, and just as nimble.

YOU MUST BE JOKING!
Knights wore padded underclothes to protect their skin from bruises and scratchy metal armor. Even with someone helping, it could take hours for a knight to get dressed and ready for battle.

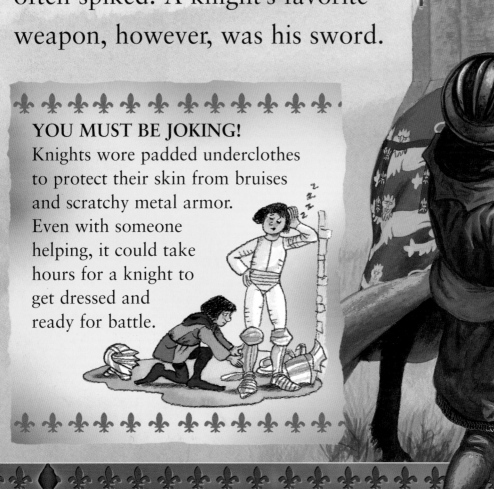

HEAVY METAL STYLES

Over the years, armor changed just as much as castles. Early knights wore chainmail, which was made by linking hundreds of small metal rings together. By the 15th century, a knight was covered from head to toe in a suit made of plate metal.

13th century   14th century   15th century

CAN YOU BELIEVE IT?
Armor made a knight so heavy, he had to be winched on to his horse by a crane.

NO. A knight's armor wasn't as heavy as it looked. He could easily climb on his horse by himself.

WHEN KNIGHTS weren't fighting real battles, there was nothing they liked better than playing war games. Tournaments were mock battles, in which knights split into two teams to fight each other.

A defeated knight had to give up his horse and armor to the winner, or pay a ransom for their return. One-to-one fights called jousts were introduced during the 13th century.

CAN YOU BELIEVE IT?
Jousting lances always had blunted tips.

NO. Sometimes knights jousted with real weapons. War games often ended in death.

Jousting for position
In a joust, two mounted knights carrying lances would charge toward each other and try to knock their opponent off his horse. A barrier called a tilt separated the knights and their horses.

YOU MUST BE JOKING!

Trainee knights called squires practised jousting by charging at a target called a quintain. When the squire hit the quintain, a heavy weight swung toward him. If his reactions weren't quick enough, it knocked him off his horse!

HUNTING AND HAWKING

When knights weren't fighting war games, their favorite sport was hunting. Special hunting dogs were used to sniff out large wild animals such as boar and bears. Birds of prey were trained to catch smaller game, such as birds, hares and rabbits.

KNIGHT SCHOOLING

USUALLY, ONLY THE SON of a lord or a knight could train to become one. Knights didn't go to a special school, though. Instead, their training began when they were about seven years old. Each boy was sent away to live in another lord's household, where he would start as a page – waiting on the lord and his lady, serving them at meals, and learning knightly behavior and good manners.

Practice makes perfect
A page was also taught how to ride and, as he became older, how to fight. He would learn to shoot a bow and arrow, and practise swordplay with a wooden sword.

YOU MUST BE JOKING!
Knightly good behavior was called chivalry, and it included treating people courteously – particularly women. In real life, knights often found it hard to live up to this ideal.

FROM SQUIRE TO KNIGHT

When he was about 14, a page would be apprenticed to a knight as his squire. If all went well, he would be made a knight when he was 21 or so. This happened at a special dubbing ceremony, during which the king or lord tapped him on the shoulder with a sword.

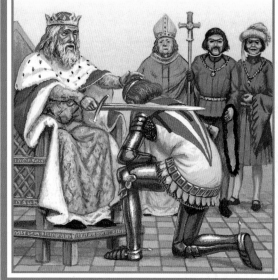

CAN YOU BELIEVE IT?
Squires rode into battle with their masters.

YES. Sometimes a squire would be knighted on the battlefield, for his bravery.

THE GREAT HALL

LIVING IN A CASTLE wasn't all about war and fighting, and the heart of daily life was the great hall. This was where everyone gathered to eat, and where the lord carried out any business to do with running the castle or his lands. In the days of castle keeps, it was also where most people, apart from the lord and his family, slept – stretched out on scratchy straw mattresses.

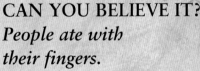

CAN YOU BELIEVE IT?
People ate with their fingers.

YES. They also used knives and spoons, but forks weren't introduced until toward the end of castle times.

YOU MUST BE JOKING!

Some lords had their own entertainer called a jester. He was rather like a clown, and his job was to make people laugh by playing tricks and telling jokes. Often he wore a special cap with bells on.

Pecking order
The lord and other important people sat at the high table, on a raised dais at one end of the great hall. The very wealthy had metal or wooden plates, but most people made do with a flat piece of stale bread called a trencher.

COMMAND PERFORMANCES

The main entertainment in the great hall was provided by musicians, or by a minstrel who played and sang. Sometimes the tables would be cleared away and people would dance. Or they would watch jugglers and acrobats, or a play put on by traveling actors.

COOKING WAS HOT, sweaty work in castle times. Most food was cooked over a huge blazing fire – everything from stews to puddings was boiled in huge metal pots called cauldrons, which hung down over the flames. If meat wasn't stewed, it was roasted over the fire on a hand-turned spit. Bread and pies were baked in an oven, which was often built into the wall beside the main fireplace.

Spitting fire
It was often the kitchen-lad's job to turn the spit. If he was lucky, he could shelter from the heat behind a screen. All the kitchen work was done by men, and the castle cook was king of his kitchen.

THE CASTLE MENU
Larger castles had their own vegetable gardens, but others were supplied with fruit and vegetables by the peasants who farmed the land around the castle. Cattle, pigs and sheep were kept for their milk and meat, and hunting parties sometimes brought back deer, wild boar and pheasants.

CAN YOU BELIEVE IT?
Dishes were cleaned in washing-up liquid.

NO. Sand was used for cleaning, or soapy herbs such as soapwort.

YOU MUST BE JOKING!
Fancy food was served up at feasts. Guests might be offered eels, tiny larks' tongues, and exotic birds such as peacocks, herons or swans.

THE LORD'S PRIVATE ROOM was called the great chamber, and it was more than a bedroom. The lord's wife, the lady, spent much of her day here. This was where she met visitors and gave orders to the steward, the man who managed the castle household. The great chamber was also a private space, where the lady and her ladies-in-waiting would embroider, make music or play chess.

Cool towers
Even though over time castles grew more comfortable, life was still chilly. The only heat came from an open fire.

YOU MUST BE JOKING!
Apart from the lady and her ladies-in-waiting, not many women lived in castles. Most of the jobs were done by men servants – although women did the laundry.

WASTE COLLECTION

Latrines were called garderobes and they were built into the castle walls – everything dropped down into the moat or a cesspit. The smelly job of cleaning out the cesspits was done by men called gong farmers.

CAN YOU BELIEVE IT?
Castles didn't have bathrooms.

YES. Only the very rich took baths, but not often and not in special bathrooms. They sat and soaked in a wooden tub in their chamber instead.

FASHIONS CAME and went during the 500 years of the castle age, but styles changed more slowly than they do today. During the 11th and 12th centuries, both men and women wore an undertunic beneath a belted overtunic.

Early 12th century

CAN YOU BELIEVE IT?
Women wore make-up.

YES. Some used white paint to lighten their skin, and wore colored eye shadow.

Women's clothes were always long, but men's might be anything from short to ankle-length. As time went on, wealthy people's clothes became tighter-fitting and more elaborate.

15th century

TURNING HEADS
In the early years, women covered their hair with a veil, or wore a cap-shaped hat with a wimple (a cloth that covered the neck). As time passed, women's headdresses became more and more complicated – some looked like animals' horns!

Ringing the changes
By the late 15th century, fashionable ladies were wearing a high-waisted gown, often trimmed with fur. Wealthy men had replaced their overtunic with a short padded doublet.

RELIGION PLAYED a very important part in people's lives during castle times, and a priest called the chaplain was a key member of the castle household. Many lords had a small private chapel near to their chamber. Often there was also a larger chapel in the castle courtyard, where the rest of the household gathered to pray.

YOU MUST BE JOKING!
Chivalrous knights were supposed to love God and be ready to die defending their faith. A squire spent the whole night before he was dubbed a knight in the chapel, praying for God's help to meet this ideal.

CAN YOU BELIEVE IT?
The chaplain often looked after the castle documents.

YES. Apart from priests, few people could read and write in castle times.

Private prayers
The lord and lady often began the day with prayers in their private chapel. It was one of the castle's most beautifully decorated rooms, with paintings and stained-glass windows.

HOLY JOURNEYS
People proved their faith in castle times by going on a journey called a pilgrimage to a holy place, such as a saint's shrine.

In the late 14th century, the English writer Geoffrey Chaucer described a pilgrimage in his *Canterbury Tales*. The pilgrims included a knight and a squire.

EUROPE WASN'T the only part of the world with lords, knights and castles. Japanese knights were called samurai, and they also wore armor and fought on horseback. A samurai's prize weapons were two long curved swords. Castles were built in Japan, too, although the finest were constructed in the 16th and 17th centuries, after the great age of castle building ended in Europe.

Eastern keep
The keep of a Japanese castle was several stories high, and each storey had its own overhanging roof. The keep was made from wood, although the basement was protected by thick stone walls.

YOU MUST BE JOKING! Some of the fortified towns built by the Anasazi people of North America were like a cross between a castle and an apartment block. The biggest, Pueblo Bonito, probably had about 600 or 700 rooms.

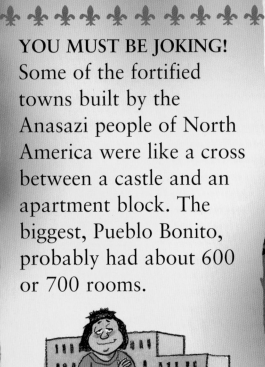

FAIRYTALE CASTLES
European castle-building didn't stop completely when the great age of castle-building ended in the 15th century. Later castles were used mainly as homes, however, and they weren't so heavily fortified. One of the most beautiful later castles was Neuschwanstein, built in the 19th century for King Ludwig of Bavaria.

CAN YOU BELIEVE IT?
All European castles were built of stone.

NO. Later ones were often made of brick.

INDEX